THE COOKING OF

Brazil

Super
Chef

MATTHEW LOCRICCHIO

WITH PHOTOS BY

JACK MCCONNELL

BENCHMARK BOOKS

MARSHALL CAVENDISH
NEW YORK

*This book is dedicated to my father Paul P. and brother Joseph J. Locricchio,
both innovative restaurant owners who demanded excellence
from all who worked for them.*

ACKNOWLEDGMENTS

Cookbooks require dedication and teamwork, and I am very lucky to be supported by both. I am deeply grateful to Maria Baez Kijac, author of *The South American Table*, for generously sharing her knowledge of the cooking of Brazil, and to the invaluable Margarida Nogueira of Rio de Janeiro, whose recipe research helped shape this book. My unending gratitude to the members of the Superchef Recipe Testers Club and their adult assistant chefs whose testing, comments, and suggestions are invaluable, especially Vicki Navratil and the excellent Steven Kosovac of Hudson, New York. Also thanks to Phyliss Tela for the loan of items from her collection used in photographing our recipes. My sincere thanks to my editor, Doug Sanders, Anahid Hamparian for her exceptional art direction, Jack McConnell for his brilliant photography, the inexhaustible Marie Hirchfeld for her exquisite food styling, and Dr. Archie Karfly for his continued support and help.

Benchmark Books
Marshall Cavendish
99 White Plains Road
Tarrytown, New York 10591-9001
www.marshallcavendish.com

Text copyright © 2005 by Matthew Locricchio
Food photographs © 2005 Jack McConnell, McConnell, McNamara & Company
Art director for food photography: Matthew Locricchio
Map copyright © 2005 by Mike Reagan

Illustrations by Janet Hamlin
Illustrations copyright © 2005 by Marshall Cavendish Corporation

Series design by Anahid Hamparian
Food styling by Marie Hirschfeld and Matthew Locricchio

Library of Congress Cataloging-in-Publication Data

Locricchio, Matthew.
The cooking of Brazil / by Matthew Locricchio.
p. cm. — (Superchef)
Includes index.
ISBN 0-7614-1732-X
1. Cookery, Brazilian. 2. Cookery—Brazil. I. Title. II. Series.

TX716.B6L63 2004
641.5981--dc22
2004010639

Photo research by Rose Corbett Gordon, Mystic, CT
Photo credits: Richard T. Nowitz/Corbis:12. Will & Deni McIntyre/Getty Images: 14.

Printed in Italy
1   3   5   6   4   2

Contents

BEFORE YOU BEGIN   6
    A Word about Safety   6
    Cooking Terms   8

THE REGIONS OF BRAZIL AND HOW THEY TASTE   10

SOUPS & STOCKS   17
    Chicken Soup   19
    Chicken Stock   22
    Black Bean Soup   25

SALADS & APPETIZERS   27
    Fresh Shrimp and Black-Eyed Pea Salad   29
    Hearts of Palm Salad   32
    Cheese Rolls   35
    Miniature Meat Pies   39

VEGETABLES & SIDE DISHES   43
    Sautéed Greens   45
    Brazilian Rice   47
    Black Beans   48
    Pepper and Lemon/Lime Sauce   50
    Brazilian Flavored Oil   51

MAIN DISHES   53
    Colonial Chicken   55
    Smoked Meat and Black Bean Stew   59
    Roasted Pork Tenderloin   62
    Fish and Shrimp Stew   65

DESSERTS   69
    Brazil Nut Cookies   70
    Brazilian Birthday Candies   72

HELPFUL KITCHEN EQUIPMENT AND UTENSILS   74
ESSENTIAL INGREDIENTS IN THE BRAZILIAN KITCHEN   76
INDEX   78
METRIC CONVERSION CHART   79

DEAR READER,

I WILL ALWAYS REMEMBER THE AROMA OF ONIONS, CELERY, AND BELL PEPPER COOKING IN MY MOTHER'S CAST-IRON DUTCH OVEN. THAT APPETIZING AROMA PERMEATES MY CHILDHOOD MEMORIES AS IT DID OUR HOME. ONE OF THE MOST DELIGHTFUL THINGS I HAVE LEARNED AS A CHEF IS HOW DEEPLY FOOD INFLUENCES OUR LIVES. FOOD TOUCHES PEOPLE ON SO MANY LEVELS—PHYSICALLY, EMOTIONALLY, SOCIALLY, AND SPIRITUALLY. THE PUBLIC'S INTEREST IN FOOD AND CUISINE IS INSATIABLE, AND I AM CONSTANTLY AMAZED AT THE LEVEL OF INTEREST AND KNOWLEDGE I SEE IN YOUNG PEOPLE. THE CUISINES OF THE WORLD ARE WIDE AND VARIED AND GIVE US A GOOD PICTURE OF HUMAN NATURE AT ITS BEST. A STUDY OF THE WORLD'S MANY DIFFERENT CUISINES UNVEILS THE RICH TAPESTRY OF CULTURAL DIFFERENCES, YET IN THE END WE LEARN ONE OF LIFE'S MOST VALUABLE LESSONS: FOOD BRINGS PEOPLE TOGETHER.

THESE COOKBOOKS, WHICH I HEARTILY ENDORSE, GIVE YOUNG PEOPLE THE CHANCE TO EXPLORE, TO CREATE, AND TO LEARN. IN **Superchef**, YOUNG READERS CAN USE THEIR HOME KITCHENS TO EXPLORE THE MANY DIFFERENT TASTES OF THE WORLD. THEY CAN LEARN THE VALUE OF WORKING TOGETHER WITH FAMILY MEMBERS IN THE HOME AND EXPERIENCE THE SHEER PLEASURE OF A PERFECT MEAL. WHEN THE CUTTING, CHOPPING, AND COOKING ARE OVER, IT'S TIME TO SIT DOWN TOGETHER AND ENJOY THE FRUITS OF THE ASPIRING CHEF'S LABOR. THIS IS WHEN YOUNG CHEFS CAN LEARN THE **REAL** SECRET OF THE GREAT CHEFS—THE JOY OF SHARING.

CHEF FRANK BRIGTSEN

BRIGTSEN'S RESTAURANT
NEW ORLEANS, LOUISIANA

From the Author

Welcome to **Superchef**. This series of cookbooks brings you traditional recipes from other countries, adapted to work in your kitchen. My goal is to introduce you to a world of exciting and satisfying recipes, along with the basic principles of kitchen safety, food handling, and common-sense nutrition. Inside you will find classic recipes from Brazil. The recipes are not necessarily all low-fat or low-calorie, but they are all healthful. Even if you are a vegetarian, you will find recipes without meat or with suggestions to make the dish meatless.

Many people today eat lots of fast food and processed or convenience foods because they are "quick and easy." As a result there are many people both young and old who simply don't know how to cook and have never experienced the pleasure of preparing a successful meal. **Superchef** can change the way you feel about cooking. You can learn to make authentic and delicious dishes from recipes that have been tested by young cooks in kitchens like yours. The recipes range from very basic to challenging. The instructions take you through the preparation of each dish step by step. Once you learn the basic techniques of the recipes, you will understand the principles of cooking fresh food successfully.

There is no better way to get to know people than to share a meal with them. Today, more than ever, it is essential to understand the many cultures that inhabit our planet. One way to really learn about a country is to know how its food tastes. You'll also be discovering the people of other countries while learning to prepare their classic recipes.

Learning to cook takes practice, patience, and common sense, but it's not nuclear science. Cooking certainly has its rewards. Just the simple act of preparing food can lift your spirits. Nothing brings family and friends together better than cooking and then sharing the meal you made. It can be fun, and you get to eat your mistakes. It can even lead to a high-paying career. Most importantly, you can be proud to say, "Oh, glad you liked it. I did it myself."

See you in the kitchen!

Matthew Locricchio

Before You Begin

A WORD ABOUT SAFETY

Safety and common sense are the two most important ingredients in any recipe. Before you begin to make the recipes in this book, take a few minutes to master some simple kitchen safety rules.

- ✔ *Ask an adult to be your assistant chef. To ensure your safety, some steps in a recipe are best done with the help of an adult, like handling pots of boiling water or hot cooking oils. Good cooking is about teamwork. With an adult assistant to help, you've got the makings of a perfect team.*

- ✔ *Read the entire recipe before you start to prepare it, and have a clear understanding of how the recipe works. If something is not clear, ask your teammate to explain it.*

- ✔ *Dress the part of a chef. Wear an apron. Tie back long hair so that it's out of your food and away from open flames. Why not do what a chef does and wear a clean hat to cover your hair!*

- ✔ *Always start with clean hands and a clean kitchen before you begin any recipe. Leave the kitchen clean when you're done.*

- ✔ *Pot holders and hot pads are your friends. The hands they save may be your own. Use them only if they are dry. Using wet holders on a hot pot can cause a serious burn!*

- ✔ *Keep the handles of the pots and pans turned toward the middle of the stove. That way you won't accidentally hit them and knock over pots of hot food. Always use pot holders to open or move a pan on the stove or in the oven.*

✔ *Remember to turn off the stove and oven when you are finished cooking. Sounds like a simple idea, but it's easy to forget.*

BE SHARP ABOUT KNIVES

✔ *A simple rule about knife safety is that your hands work as a team. One hand grips the handle and operates the knife while the other guides the food you are cutting. The hand holding the food should never come close to the blade of the knife. Keep the fingertips that hold the food slightly curved and out of the path of the blade, and use your thumb to keep the food steady. Go slowly. There is no reason to chop very fast.*

✔ *Always hold the knife handle with **dry** hands. If your hands are wet, the knife might slip. Work on a cutting board, never a tabletop or countertop.*

✔ *Never place sharp knives in a sink full of soapy water, where they could be hidden from view. Someone reaching into the water might get hurt.*

✔ *Take good care of your knives. Good chef knives should be washed by hand, never in a dishwasher.*

COOKING TERMS

Brazilian cooking fuses the culinary identities of cultures spanning three continents. By combining Brazil's basic native Indian culinary roots with African food artistry and Portuguese spices and ingredients, a national cuisine was born. One of the most appealing things about the cooking of Brazil is that the recipes are not overly complicated. Some involve extra steps that can be time consuming, but any extra effort spent preparing a dish will be greatly rewarded with the surprisingly delicious results. Here are a few simple techniques for you to follow as you discover the cooking of Brazil.

Grate *To grate means to finely shred foods. A four-sided metal grater with a handle at the top will give you a place to hold on to as you work. Always use extreme caution when using a grater and don't allow your fingers to come too close to the grating surface.*

Sauté *To lightly fry ingredients in a small amount of fat, butter, or oil, while stirring with a spoon or spatula.*

Simmer   *To cook food in a liquid kept just below the boiling point. Gentle bubbles will roll lazily to the top of a liquid that is simmering. Simmering is an important part of Brazilian cooking and is used in the long, slow cooking of beans, soups, stews, and braised meats.*

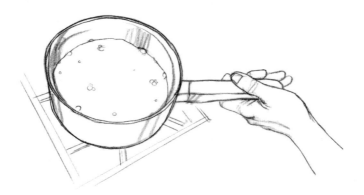

Skim   *Fats or impurities will rise to the surface of simmering or boiling soups or sauces. Skimming removes these unwanted residues as well as reduces fat and enriches flavor. Use a large metal spoon or small ladle to remove and discard them.*

The Regions of Brazil and How They Taste

The cooking of Brazil stands apart from all other South American cuisines because of its unique ingredients and flavors. Brazil's fascinating mixture of cultures, which blends native Indian, Portugese, and African influences, has informed and shaped its national cuisine.

The cooking of Brazil began to differ drastically from all other South American cuisines more than 500 years ago when Portuguese colonists brought the first slaves to Brazil from Africa. Many of the transplanted African women who ran the kitchens of the colonists were experts at cooking over open fires, baking, and using spices. They invented new recipes by combining familiar elements from their homelands with the wide assortment of local ingredients that native residents used in their everyday dishes. In addition, the Portuguese brought to this vast unknown country the ingredients that most reminded them of home—items such as salt, sugar, spices, eggs, and vinegar. Through the years, Amerindian dishes absorbed the influence of African and Portugese cuisine. In later centuries, as a result of immigration from other parts of Europe, German, Italian, and eastern European influences had their impact as well. What resulted was a diverse medley of ingredients and techniques which, like any good recipe, came together in new and exciting ways. Despite this widespread diversity and cultural variety, from a culinary perspective, the nation can be divided into two distinct regions, the north and the south. Each region bursts with its own flavors and long culinary traditions just waiting to be shared.

THE SOUTH

The southern states of Minas Gerais, Espírito Santo, Rio de Janeiro, and São Paulo are home to more than 90 percent of the nation's population. The southeast is also the most industrialized part of the country. Nearly 7 million people live in the city of Rio de Janeiro, which was the capital of Brazil until 1960. Rio, as it is often called, is densely inhabited and a city of opposites, where poverty and luxury live side by side.

Rio has one of the most dazzling settings of any city in the world with the Atlantic on the east and dramatic highlands to the west. It is especially famous for the festival of Carnival, a national holiday, when the city throws a sprawling five-day party before the beginning of Lent on Ash Wednesday. Huge, eye-popping floats tower over the streets rolling past revelers in glittering costumes dancing to the samba and lambada beats. With such a festive atmosphere is it any wonder that Brazilians call their hometown *Cidade Maravilhosa,* or "marvelous city"?

Rio is also known for one of its Saturday traditions. In years past, the resourceful African slaves began making a dish with leftover cuts of meat that were considered undesirable and didn't appeal to the colonists they were cooking for. Rather than waste this meat, they cooked it with black beans, onions, garlic, and assorted spices. The fragrance of

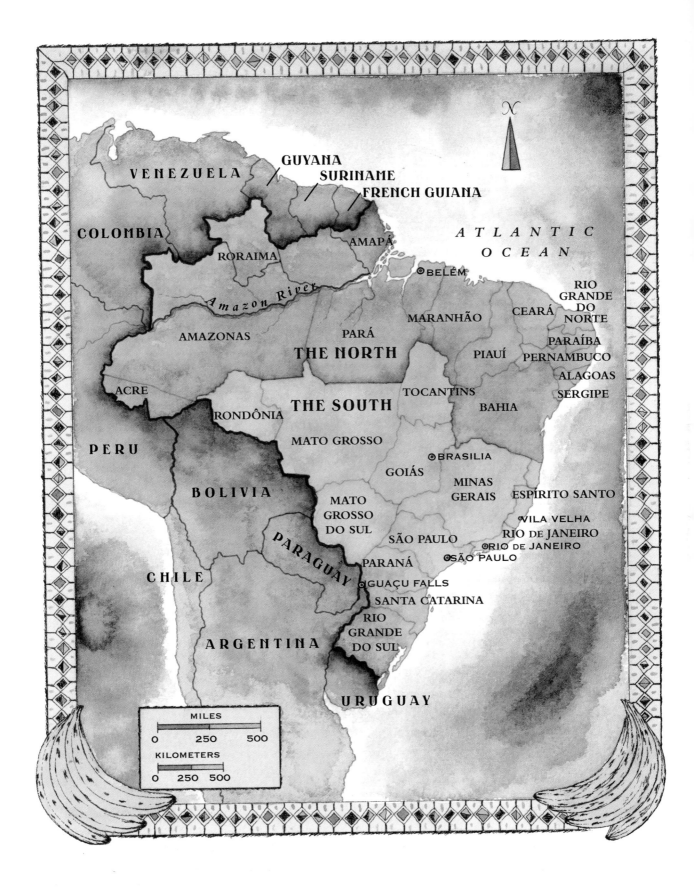

Late afternoon shadows creep across the downtown precincts of Rio de Janeiro, a city known for its dramatic coastal setting.

the simmering dish filled the plantation houses. Once the landowners began to smell and eventually taste this delicious creation, they wanted to share it as well. Thus the national dish, *feijoada completa*, was born. The meal begins with a delicious black bean soup. Then sautéed collard greens or kale, delicate cheese rolls, Brazilian rice, and platters of fresh sliced oranges are served along with the smoked and fresh pork, beef, sausages, and richly flavored black beans that make up the *feijoada completa*. A complete feast! Diners return several times to select from the artfully displayed platters of ingredients, choosing their favorites and enjoying them at a leisurely pace.

Despite its massive population, Rio is not Brazil's largest city. That distinction belongs to São Paulo—a name that lends itself not only to a city, but also to the state that contains it. São Paulo is 120 miles south of Rio and is home to almost 18 million people. It is South America's richest state. The cosmopolitan city of São Paulo contains some of the most innovative architecture in the world. There is even a hotel built in the shape of a giant slice of watermelon.

São Paulo was first settled 450 years ago by Jesuit missionaries. Today the city is composed of ultramodern skyscrapers, brick factories, tenements, and gleaming residential apartments. It is a center of Brazilian art and music. The ethnic diversity the city is known for makes it home to every kind of cuisine imaginable. As a result, *Paulistos*, as the city residents are called, are experts at selecting good food. One local favorite is a salad made with dried cod, a Brazilian specialty with Portugese origins.

To escape the fast pace and heat of the cities, *Cariocas*, the residents of Rio, and *Paulistos* head north to the state of Espírito Santo and the beaches at Vila Velha, first colonized in the sixteenth century. The seafood there is outstanding. A local fish stew, *moqueca capixaba*, made from the day's catch and simmered with fresh tomatoes, green onions, fish stock, cilantro, and lime juice is reason enough to visit.

To the west of Espírito Santo lies the expansive state of Minas Gerais. About the size of France, it was where three-quarters of the world's gold deposits were discovered around 1675 along the rivers that thread their way out of Brazil's oldest and tallest mountains, the Serra da Mantiqueira.

This state is also known for another kind of gold—cheese. Minas Gerais is the country's leading producer of milk, butter, and cheese. Many believe the best cooks in Brazil are found in Minas Gerais, and, judging by the raw materials they have to work with, it just might be true. Fruits such as pineapple, cherries, grapes, figs, passion fruit, guava, and papaya grow abundantly. Tomatoes thrive in the mineral-rich soil along with onions, peppers, peas, beets, okra, pumpkins, collard greens, kale, carrots, sugarcane, and of course the ever-present coffee bean. Brazil is the leading grower of coffee in the world.

Farmers in Minas Gerais developed a recipe many years ago that is now enjoyed all over Brazil. A loin of pork is marinated in lime, garlic, peppers, orange juice, and parsley then slow roasted to perfection. Another dish beloved throughout Brazil is a type of chicken soup, the ultimate comfort food. It is a recipe that many believe originated in Minas Gerais. Brazilians call their chicken soup, *canja,* and once you taste it you'll know why Brazilians love it.

As you travel across the southern tip of the country into the prosperous state of Paraná, you might forget you are in Brazil. The cooking and architecture found there reflect a distinct European influence. Italian and German immigrants settled there in the mid-nineteenth century. The rolling plains, or pampas, that make up Rio Grande do Sul, Brazil's southernmost state, spread far beyond the border with Argentina. This is cattle country. Cowboys, called gauchos, have led cattle drives across these grasslands since the early eighteenth century. Large numbers of Italian, German, Swiss and eastern Europeans settled there in the late nineteenth century, and the the local cuisine still reflects the influence.

The necessity of having to travel long distances on cattle drives led the gauchos to create a method of preserving meats that allowed them to carry beef with them in their saddlebags while they moved cattle from place to place. The beef was salted then dried in the sun to keep the meat from spoiling. *Carne do sol* is still popular today and is an essential ingredient in such distinctive Brazilian dishes as *feijoada.* A local dish called wagoner's rice, a blend of dried beef, rice, tomatoes, green pepper, and the incredibly hot *malagueta* chile peppers, is also a favorite.

The gauchos also used a style of cooking that is familiar in North America. When it was time to feed the large numbers of men traveling on the cattle drives, meats were cooked over open fires. They were rubbed with coarse salt or basted with simple sauces of salted water and peppers to seal in the juices and keep the beef tender. Linguica, a Brazilian sausage, slid onto long skewers, was roasted over the fire as well. The result was a style of cooking called *churrasc,* named after the long swordlike skewers. Restaurants called *churrascarias* are a meat lover's dream and are popular today throughout Brazil and the world.

Though beef remains the meat of choice in the south, chicken and pork are not

The Amazon offers up its treasures at the port city of Belém, where fishermen unload the day's catch—baskets of tiny fish to be sold in local markets.

overlooked. A favorite dish in Rio Grande do Sul, and evidence of the state's Italian culinary influence, is a chicken-and-rice combination cooked with tomatoes, garlic, and onion, then topped with a golden crust of Parmesan cheese.

For a taste of the south try: Smoked Meat and Black Bean Stew, Cheese Rolls, Sautéed Greens, Fresh Shrimp and Black-Eyed Pea Salad, Fish and Shrimp Stew, Roasted Pork Tenderloin, Brazilian Rice, and Colonial Chicken.

THE NORTH

In the north lies the Amazon River and Basin, which covers more than 50 percent of the landmass of Brazil. At 1,962 miles, the Amazon is one of the world's mighty waterways. The diversity of the ecosystem there is unequaled anywhere else on Earth. It is home to approximately 20 percent of all the plants, animals, and birds found on the planet. Rainforest plants that thrive there provide the world with about 25 percent of its medicine.

The rain forests of the Amazon Basin have been called "the earth's lungs," as they contribute to the health of the planet. Concerned people and organizations in Brazil and throughout the world work to protect the ecological health of this diverse and irreplaceable region.

Rivers are not Brazil's only aquatic resource. The country's coastal waters provide a wealth of seafood that finds its way into many local delicacies. Freshly caught fish are cooked with tropical fruits and are a specialty of the state of Pará and its capital, Belém. Fresh crabs are boiled and cracked open, and the meat is dipped in a spicy sauce of tomatoes, vinegar, onions, and chile peppers. Luscious local tropical fruits with unfamiliar names, such as guaraná, bacuri, and sapote, are also eaten fresh or enjoyed as refreshing juices.

A tropical marvel native to this region is the Brazil nut tree, an evergreen that can reach 150 feet tall and 6 feet in circumference. Have you ever seen a pinecone? Imagine one that weighs almost 5 pounds, but instead of seeds on the inside there are nuts. Brazil nuts are packed with protein and a delicious snack. They are also used in countless dishes in the region, even in cookies that combine white cornmeal, butter, and flour to create a crunchy delight.

It is the state of Bahia, however, that many Brazilians associate with outstanding cooking. The food there is quite different from that of the rest of Brazil. The African culinary influence, evident in so much of Brazilian cooking, is most noticeable in Bahia. Nuts, coconut milk, and a dark orange palm oil called *dendê* are just a few examples. This flavorful oil is used extensively in much of the local cooking, and the color and flavor it lends to dishes is distinctly Bahian. North Americans might find its highly saturated fat content reason to pass it up, but in Bahia it is an essential ingredient. *Dendê* oil is usually added at the end of cooking in order to ensure its color and flavor are at their peak.

Palm oil is not the only local ingredient that finds its way into the dishes of Bahia. Manioc, or cassava, grows abundantly in the state and throughout Brazil. Manioc remains as much a part of the cooking of Brazil today as it was when the Amerindians first used it thousands of years ago. Cooked, dried, then ground into flour or a coarse meal, it is one of the key ingredients, along with beans, fish, and rice, used in the cooking of Brazil.

Another unique vegetable featured in the cooking of Bahia is the delicate center, or heart, of young palm trees. Hearts of palm are cooked until tender, then combined with fresh oranges, cashews, and mint into a refreshing local salad. Delicate miniature pies, called *pastel de carne,* filled with a spicy, simmered, ground-meat filling, are another favorite.

A hard cheese similar to Parmesan is blended into rolls made from manioc flour. Manioc is also an essential ingredient in *farofa,* a Brazilian condiment served alongside or on top of savory dishes and similar to our salt or ground pepper. In fact a *farofa* has its own shaker called a *farinheira,* and is found on every table in Brazil. *Farofas* can be simple or elaborate. A popular one in Bahia is made with bananas and onions.

For a taste of the north try: Chicken Soup, Hearts of Palm Salad, Miniature Meat Pies, and Brazil Nut Cookies.

Now that you know something about the cooking of Brazil, your journey really begins. Put on some samba music, and start to discover what makes Brazilian food so tantalizing. Once your guests sample your dishes they are bound to say, "*Muito obrigado. A comida estava delicisa!*" ("Thank you very much. The food was delicious!")

Soups
&
Stocks

From left: Black Bean Soup (page 25)
Cheese Rolls (page 35), and Chicken Soup
(page 19)

Chicken Soup *Canja de Galinha*

There is nothing as comforting as chicken soup. *Canja*, with countless versions and variations, is served all over Brazil and is regarded as one of the national dishes. Brazilians fell in love with this soup almost 500 years ago, when the Portuguese first introduced them to rice. This recipe involves some extra steps, which are not part of most soup recipes. Making your own chicken soup is worth all the effort that goes into it, though, and it's a great way to make new friends. Everyone will want a bowlful.

Serves 6

Ingredients

1 3½-pound chicken, cut into 8 pieces,
    preferably organic
2 tablespoons vegetable oil
2 cloves garlic
2 teaspoons salt
1 medium onion
1 whole clove

1 large carrot
1 bay leaf
½ teaspoon freshly ground black pepper
10 cups water
½ cup long-grain rice
5 sprigs fresh mint

On your mark . . .

- **Wash the chicken pieces, pat them dry with a paper towel, and lay them in a large bowl.**
- **Wash your hands with lots of hot soapy water.**
- **Lay the garlic cloves on a cutting board and slightly crush them with the flat side of a knife. Cut off the stem end and discard it. Roughly chop the garlic.**
- **Sprinkle the salt over the chopped garlic and mash it with a fork. Continue to mash until the garlic and salt combine into a paste.**
- **Add the garlic-and-salt combination to the chicken pieces.**
- **Toss well with a spoon to coat the chicken with the paste, cover with foil, and refrigerate for up to 2 hours to marinate.**

Get set . . .

- **Just before the chicken has finished marinating, prepare the rest of the ingredients.**
- **Press the clove into the skin of the onion. You will cook the onion whole in the soup.**
- **Wash and peel the carrot and set aside.**

Cook!

- Remove the chicken from the refrigerator.
- Heat the oil in a heavy-bottomed pan large enough to hold all the ingredients. A Dutch oven or soup pot will work best.
- Once the oil is hot but not smoking, brown the chicken pieces on both sides. You will have to do this in two batches, as there won't be enough room in the pan to cook all the pieces at once.

- Remove the browned pieces to a clean platter, and ask your adult assistant to drain the fat from the pot. Leave the browned bits stuck to the bottom of the pot, they will add additional flavor to the soup.
- Return the chicken to the pot along with the onion, carrot, bay leaf, black pepper, and the water and bring it to a boil over high heat. This will take 15 to 20 minutes.

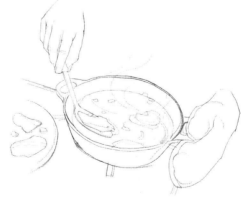

- Once it boils, reduce the heat to low, cover the pot leaving the lid slightly ajar, and cook for 1½ hours, or until the chicken is cooked through and tender.
- Several times during cooking carefully skim the foam or fat that rises to the top.
- When the chicken is done, turn off the heat. Ask your adult assistant to remove the chicken pieces and the carrot from the broth with a slotted spoon and lay

them on a clean tray or platter to cool. Discard the onion.

- Pour the broth through a fine mesh strainer into a heat-proof bowl or pan, then pour it back into the pot it was just cooked in.

- Return the broth to a boil over high heat, then add the rice, and 1 teaspoon salt.
- As soon as the broth boils again, reduce the heat to low and cook uncovered for 15 minutes or until the rice is tender.
- In the meantime, remove the skin from the chicken and discard. Pull the meat off the bones and tear it into medium-size pieces. Discard the chicken bones.

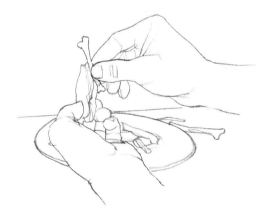

- Slice the carrot into small cubes, then add the chicken and carrots to the pan. Heat the soup through for 5 minutes.
- In the meantime, wash the mint, remove the leaves from the stems, and tear the leaves in half.
- Serve the soup hot and garnish each bowl with a few of the mint leaves.

Chicken Stock *Caldo de Galinha*

Give this recipe a try and experience what Brazilian cooks already know. Homemade chicken stock not only tastes better than canned, it gives recipes the authentic flavor of Brazil.

Makes about 1/2 gallon

Ingredients

3 1/2 to 4 pounds chicken wings, preferably organic
2 medium onions
10 to 12 sprigs flat-leaf parsley
2 carrots, unpeeled
2 stalks celery

3 whole garlic cloves, unpeeled
10 black peppercorns
2 bay leaves
6 to 8 whole cloves
6 quarts cold water

On your mark . . .

- **Put the chicken pieces in a colander, rinse thoroughly with cold water, and allow to drain as you prepare the rest of the ingredients.**

Get set . . .

- **Cut the onions in half without peeling them, and add them to a pot large enough to hold all the ingredients.**
- **Wash the parsley thoroughly, shake off the excess water, chop it roughly, and add it to the onions in the pot.**
- **Scrub the carrots with a vegetable brush to remove any dirt but do not peel. Cut them into large chunks and add them to the pot.**
- **Wash the celery, cut it into large pieces, and add them to the pot as well.**
- **Add the garlic cloves, along with the peppercorns, bay leaves, and cloves.**

Cook!

- **Place the pot on the stove. Add the chicken and the water.**
- **Bring the stock to a boil over high heat. This will take about 25 to 30 minutes.**
- **Skim any foam or impurities that rise to the top.**
- **Once the stock boils, reduce the heat to simmer, and cook for 2 hours.**
- **Continue to skim the stock as it cooks. Turn off the heat and let the stock stand for about 10 minutes.**

- Ask your adult assistant to drain it through a fine mesh sieve or colander into a heat-proof bowl or large pot.
- After the solids in the sieve have cooled they can be discarded, but the cooked chicken makes a tasty snack.
- Cover and chill the stock in the refrigerator.
- Remove any fat that has hardened on the top and discard. The stock is now ready for use.

CHEF'S TIP *Chicken stock can be kept in the refrigerator tightly covered for up to 4 days, or frozen for up to 3 months. Always thaw chicken stock overnight in the refrigerator or in a saucepan on the stovetop over medium heat. Never thaw it at room temperature.*

Black Bean Soup *Sopa de Feijão*

Once you have prepared a pot of black beans, there are lots of other recipes you can make. Black Bean Soup is one of the best of them. Follow the recipe on page 48 for preparing beans. Once you have cooked the beans, or better yet the day after, follow this recipe to make one of the most popular soups in Brazil.

Serves 4 to 6

Ingredients

2 cups cooked Black Beans (page 48)
2 cups water, homemade Chicken Stock
    (page 22), or canned low-sodium chicken broth

1 hard-boiled egg
1 small bunch cilantro
4 to 5 slices bacon (optional)

On your mark, get set . . .

- Place 1 cup of the cooked beans in a blender. Add 1 cup of the water or chicken stock.
- Blend at high speed until you have the consistency of a thick cream.
- Pour the blended beans into a large saucepan.
- Pour the remaining cup of beans and liquid into the blender and blend at high speed. Add to the saucepan then set aside for the moment.
- Peel the hard-boiled egg, finely chop it, and set it aside.
- Wash the cilantro to remove any dirt. Shake off the excess water, wrap the cilantro in a paper towel to absorb any remaining moisture, then roughly chop it. Set the cilantro aside.

Cook!

- If using the bacon, place the strips in a frying pan set over medium-high heat and cook until just crispy.
- Place the bacon on paper towels to drain and let cool.
- Crumble or break the strips into small pieces and set aside.
- Place the saucepan containing the soup over medium heat. Stir the soup frequently as it cooks. Skim any foam that rises to the top.
- Be careful it does not come to a boil too quickly. If that happens, lower the heat.
- Serve hot and garnish with the chopped egg, cilantro, and the bacon bits.

Salads
&
Appetizers

From upper left: Fresh Shrimp and Black-Eyed Pea Salad (page 29) and Hearts of Palm Salad (page 32)

Fresh Shrimp and Black-Eyed Pea Salad *Salada de Feijão Fradinho com Camarão*

The cosmopolitan city of São Paulo with its dazzling architecture, vibrant street life, and art museums is also home to some of Brazil's most exciting cuisine. Restaurants serve the traditional as well as the new cuisine of some of South American's rising culinary stars. This recipe, usually prepared with dried cod or dried shrimp, is a favorite in São Paulo. This version uses fresh shrimp instead of dried, but the results are just as authentic and the taste is, too.

Serves 4

Ingredients

1 pound fresh large or fully thawed frozen shrimp
1 1/2 teaspoons salt
1 cup cold water
1 pound black-eyed peas
1 small yellow onion
1 cup bottled all-natural clam juice★
1 small red onion
1 medium red bell pepper

8 to 10 sprigs flat-leaf parsley
1 garlic clove
4 tablespoons extra-virgin olive oil
1 tablespoon white wine vinegar
5 to 6 large lettuce leaves, romaine or green or red leaf
1 lime

On your mark, get set . . .

- Carefully peel the shrimp, leaving the tails on. Discard the shells.
- Remove the vein along the back of the shrimp. To do this, lay the shrimp on a cutting board, then using a paring knife, make a slight cut about 1/4 inch deep, starting at the widest end, or the top, of the shrimp. As you cut, you will see a black vein. Rinse the shrimp under cold running water, and pull out and discard the vein. Repeat with the rest of the shrimp.
- Place the shrimp in a large bowl and add 1/2 teaspoon of the salt and the cold water. Toss the shrimp with a spoon a few times to help dissolve the salt and then refrigerate.

Cook!

- In a medium saucepan, combine the black-eyed peas and enough water to cover them by about 1 inch.
- Bring to a boil over high heat and cook for 1 minute.

- Remove the pan from the heat, cover tightly, and let soak for 1 hour.
- Peel the yellow onion, cut in half, and set aside.
- Drain the soaked black-eyed peas and return them to the pan. Add the clam juice and the onion halves and enough fresh water to cover by 1 inch.
- Bring to a boil over high heat, reduce the heat to low, and simmer until the peas are tender, about 30 to 35 minutes.
- During the last 10 minutes of cooking, add 1/2 teaspoon of salt.
- Drain the black-eyed peas and remove the onion halves. Rinse the black-eyed peas under cold running water, drain again, and let cool completely.
- In the meantime, peel the red onion, cut into small chunks, measure 3/4 cup, and set aside.
- Wash the bell pepper and cut out the stem at the top.
- Slice the pepper in half and remove the seeds and white membrane.
- Cut the pepper into thin slices, then cut the slices into small squares, measure 1 cup, and set aside.

- Wash the parsley, shaking off any excess water. Remove the stems, roughly chop the leaves, measure 1/4 cup, and set aside.
- Slightly crush the garlic by laying the flat side of a chef's knife on the clove and pressing evenly to break open the skin. Remove the skin and the root end, chop the garlic, and set aside.
- Remove the shrimp from the refrigerator and drain well, shaking the colander to remove excess water.
- Heat the olive oil in a 10-inch frying pan over medium heat for 30 to 40 seconds.
- Add the chopped red onion and sauté for 3 to 4 minutes.
- Add the garlic and bell pepper and sauté for 2 to 3 minutes.

- Add the drained shrimp, vinegar, the remaining teaspoon of salt, and the parsley and sauté until the shrimp turn bright pink and are tender and just cooked, about 2 to 3 minutes.
- Remove from the heat and let cool for 5 minutes.
- Combine the drained peas and sautéed shrimp in a large bowl. Refrigerate until completely cooled.
- Wash the lettuce leaves, shake off the excess water, drain, then pat them dry with a paper towel. Tear the leaves into medium-size pieces.

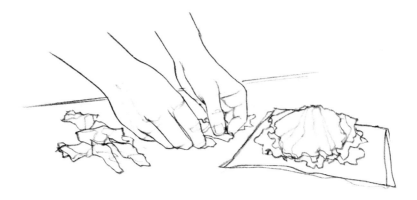

- Cut the lime into thin slices.
- Arrange the lettuce on a serving platter, then spoon on the chilled shrimp and peas.
- Garnish with fresh lime slices and serve cold.

★ *Look for clam juice with no additional salt added, otherwise omit the salt in the recipe.*

Hearts of Palm Salad
Salada de Palmito

Hearts of palm have long been a part of Brazil's cuisine. The Amerindians of the Atlantic coastal region in and around the state of Bahia first shared hearts of palm, which grow in abundance in Brazil's tropical climate, with the Portuguese colonists. This easy-to-make salad featuring this simple ingredient is uncommonly refreshing and will be the perfect accompaniment to your Brazilian meal.

Serves 4

Ingredients

1 6-ounce can hearts of palm
2 cups hot water
1 lime
3 tablespoons extra-virgin olive oil
1/2 teaspoon salt
1/4 teaspoon freshly ground black pepper
2 medium oranges, preferably organic

2 ripe medium tomatoes, preferably organic
1/2 head of lettuce, Boston, red or green leaf, or romaine, preferably organic
1/4 cup whole, unsalted cashews
4 to 5 sprigs fresh mint

On your mark, get set, chill!

- Drain the hearts of palm in a colander, and place them in a bowl. Cover them with the hot water and set them aside while you prepare the rest of the ingredients.
- Cut the lime in half. Squeeze the juice and add it to a small jar with a tight-fitting lid.
- Add the olive oil, salt, and pepper.
- Put the lid on the jar, shake well, and set aside. This is the salad dressing.
- Wash and peel the oranges, cut them into thin slices crosswise, and set aside.
- Wash the tomatoes, cut out the stem circle from the top, and dice the remaining part into small chunks. Place them in a bowl.
- Drain the hearts of palm and gently shake the colander to remove any excess moisture.
- Cut the hearts into 1/2-inch-round slices and add them to the bowl with the tomatoes.
- Shake the dressing again and pour it over the palm-and-tomato combination.
- Wash the lettuce leaves and pat them dry with paper towels.
- Arrange the lettuce leaves on a platter.
- Mound the palm-and-tomato combination in the center of the leaves.

- Arrange the orange slices and cashew nuts around the outer edge of the platter.
- Wash the fresh mint and remove the leaves from the stems.
- Garnish the salad with the mint leaves and serve cold.

Cheese Rolls *Pão de Queijo*

These delicate rolls are originally from Minas Gerais but have become so popular they can be found across the country. But be forewarned, *pão de queijo* disappear almost as soon as they come out of the oven. Once you have your first taste, you will see why these rolls rarely have the chance to get cold.

Makes 40 to 45 rolls

Ingredients

4 cups manioc starch or tapioca flour or starch★
1 teaspoon salt
4 ounces Parmesan cheese (1⅓ cups)
1 cup plus 3 tablespoons whole milk

2 tablespoons butter
3 large eggs
1 tablespoon canola oil, for forming the rolls

On your mark, get set . . .

- **Add the tapioca flour and salt to a large bowl.**
- **Blend together with a whisk.**
- **Grate the cheese using the largest holes on a box grater. Measure 1 cup and set aside.**

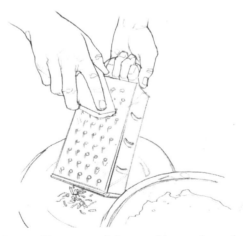

- **Measure the rest of the ingredients and have them close by.**
- **You will need an ungreased cookie sheet to bake the rolls.**

Cook!

- **Preheat the oven to 425°F.**
- **Pour 1 cup of the milk into a saucepan and add the butter. Bring to a boil over medium-high heat. Be careful the milk does not boil over.**

- Pour the milk-and-butter combination over the flour. Mix together with a fork or spoon. Let the mixture cool a bit.
- Add the eggs, one at a time, mixing each into the dough before adding the next.
- Add the final 3 tablespoons of milk to the dough, a spoonful at a time, until the dough is smooth. If the dough feels dry, add a little more milk, but no more than 1 tablespoon.

- Knead the dough in the bowl until all the ingredients are well blended and the dough is smooth.
- Add the grated cheese and mix it into the dough. Don't worry if the cheese doesn't blend in completely.
- Lightly grease the palms of your very clean hands with some of the oil.
- Tear off a piece of the dough about the size of a ping-pong ball.
- Lightly roll the dough into a ball in the palms of your hands.

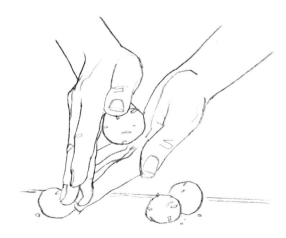

- Place it on the baking sheet.
- Repeat until all the rolls are formed and placed on the baking sheet, leaving 1/4 inch between each roll.

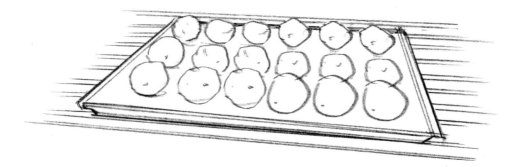

- If you need to bake the dough in two batches, refrigerate the unformed dough while the first batch bakes, or use two baking sheets.
- Bake the rolls on the middle rack of the preheated oven for 10 minutes. Set a timer so you don't forget.
- **Reduce the heat to 375°F and bake an additional 10 to 15 minutes, or until the rolls are a light golden brown.**
- Remove the rolls from the oven and lift them with a pair of tongs or a spatula to a cooling rack. Serve warm.

★ *Manioc, cassava, or tapioca flour or starch are the same ingredient just identified with different names. Tapioca starch or flour is available in health-food stores. You are most likely to find it with the wheat-free or gluten-free products. Read more about manioc in the Essential Ingredients (page 77).*

Miniature Meat Pies *Pastel de Carne*

For something so small, these tiny pies have achieved star status in the region of Bahia. Baked *pastel* are served as appetizers or snacks. The fillings vary depending on the region, but one thing is consistent—pastels are outrageously delicious. When preparing this recipe, you can use a food processor to make the pastry. Ask your adult assistant to help with that step. Or the pastry can be made by hand.

Makes about 34 mini pies

Ingredients

The Pastry
3 cups all-purpose flour
1 teaspoon salt
1/2 stick very cold unsalted butter (2 ounces)
2 eggs
3 tablespoons vegetable oil
1/4 cup ice water

The Filling
1 small yellow onion
2 garlic cloves
2 tablespoons extra-virgin olive oil
1 pound ground beef round or sirloin
8 to 10 sprigs flat-leaf parsley
1 teaspoon ground cumin
1/2 teaspoon paprika
1/2 teaspoon salt
1 cup tomato sauce or tomato salsa
5 to 6 drops Tabasco sauce or to taste
1/4 cup grated Parmesan cheese
10 green olives stuffed with pimento

On your mark . . .

- To make the pastry in a food processor, follow the manufacturer's instructions for making pie crust but use the ingredients listed above.
- Dust the ball of dough with a little flour, cover it in plastic wrap, and refrigerate for 1 hour or overnight.
- To make the pastry by hand, place the flour and salt together in a large bowl, and whisk to blend them together.
- Carefully cut the cold butter into small chunks and add to the flour in the bowl.
- Using a pastry cutter, or the tips of your very clean fingers, combine the butter and flour together into a coarse, crumbly mixture.

- Work quickly to keep the butter cold. Don't worry if the butter is not fully combined with the flour, it should be the size of small peas.
- Add the egg and vegetable oil and, using the pastry cutter or a fork, combine the ingredients. Add a little of the ice water and mix well.
- Slowly add the remaining water and continue to mix until you can press the dough into a ball.
- Place the dough onto a lightly floured countertop and knead it a few times. Be careful not to overwork the dough.
- Dust the ball of dough with a little flour, seal it in a plastic bag, or wrap it and refrigerate it for 1 hour or overnight.

Get set . . .

- To make the filling, peel the onion, chop it into small pieces, measure 3/4 to 1 cup, and set aside.
- Slightly crush the garlic by laying the flat side of a chef's knife on the clove and pressing evenly to break open the skin. Remove the skin, cut off the root end, and chop the garlic. Measure 1 tablespoon and set it aside.
- Wash the parsley to remove any dirt, shake off the excess water, and then roll it in a paper towel to blot any remaining moisture. Remove the stems, finely chop the leaves, measure 1/4 cup, and set aside.

Cook!

- Heat the oil in a 10-inch frying pan over medium heat for 30 to 40 seconds.
- When the oil is hot but not smoking, add the onions and garlic, and sauté for 2 to 3 minutes.
- Add the ground beef, chopped parsley, cumin, paprika, salt, pepper, tomato sauce, and Tabasco, if using it.
- Break the meat up with a metal spoon as you mix the ingredients together. This is a slow process so be patient.
- Reduce the heat to low and cook for 10 minutes. Stir occasionally to keep the beef from sticking, and maintain enough heat to keep the liquid at a simmer as it cooks.
- Once the meat has cooked and most of the liquid has reduced, pour the filling into a heat-proof bowl.
- Put the olives into a hand strainer or colander and rinse with cold water. Chop the olives and add them to the filling along with the grated cheese.
- Let the filling cool while you roll out the pastry.
- **Preheat the oven to 400° F.**

- Lightly grease a mini-muffin tin (24 1¾-by-1-inch muffin cups) with butter.
- To do this, tear off a square piece of wax paper and spread a little butter on. Rub the inside of each muffin cup with the buttered wax paper.
- Remove the pastry from the refrigerator.
- Lightly flour a rolling pin and sprinkle a little flour on a clean countertop.
- Cut the pastry into three sections. Cover and refrigerate two sections of the pastry while you roll out the first.
- Roll the pastry out with the rolling pin, flipping it over occasionally, until it is about 1/8 inch thick.
- Continue to lightly dust the rolling pin with small amounts of flour, but only if the pastry is sticking.
- Using a 3-inch round cookie cutter or a clean, empty soup can from which you have removed the lid on one end, cut the pastry into circles. To do this press the cutter into the pastry, but don't twist it.
- Keep the circles right next to each other as indicated by the illustration.

- Pull up one circle of the cut dough, and lay it into the muffin tin. Gently push it down into the cup.
- Repeat until all the circles are cut, and the cups are filled.
- Add a teaspoon of the filling into the pastry cup.
- Gently press the top edge of the pastry around the filling being careful not to seal it.
- Repeat until all the pastry cups are filled.
- Set the tin on the middle rack of the preheated oven and bake for 25 minutes or until golden brown.
- Remove the pies from the oven and let cool for 5 to 10 minutes, and then lift them out of the tin and let them cool on a rack.
- Serve warm or at room temperature.

CHEF'S TIP *The leftover pastry should not be rerolled to make additional pastry cups. It will become too tough from being overworked.*

Vegetables & Side Dishes

Clockwise from upper left: Black Beans (page 48), Brazilian Rice (page 47), Pepper and Lemon/Lime Sauce (page 50), and Sautéed Greens (page 45)

Sautéed Greens *Couve à Mineira*

The simplest ingredients can be transformed into the most delectable of dishes in the hands of the Brazilian cook, as this recipe from the state of Minas Gerais demonstrates.

Serves 4

Ingredients

1 pound collard greens, kale, or green or red Swiss chard

1 tablespoon bacon fat or vegetable oil
1 teaspoon salt (or to taste)

On your mark, get set . . .

- Wash the greens in a sink full of cold water until no grit or sand remains. Remove any dark or discolored spots or shriveled edges.
- Take one leaf at a time and lay it on a cutting board.
- Using the tip of a sharp knife, cut the leaves away from the tough stem that runs up the center. Discard the stem.
- Lay the leaves aside, stacked on top of each other, and continue until all the stems have been removed.
- Tightly roll all the leaves together into a long cigar shape.
- Take your time doing this. If the pile is too big, divide it in half.
- After the leaves have been rolled into a tight cigar shape, slice them crosswise into very thin strips, the thinner the better. Be patient, this is a slow process so don't rush it.
- Once all the leaves have been cut into thin ribbons, gently toss them a few times to loosen them, and then set them aside for the moment.
- If your hand gets tired, it is all right to let the leaves unroll and take a rest. Just reroll them when you are ready to continue.

Cook!

- Heat the bacon fat or oil in a 10-inch frying pan over medium-high heat for 30 to 40 seconds.
- Once the oil is hot but not smoking, add the greens and sprinkle them with the salt.
- Sauté quickly until the greens have absorbed some of the oil and have turned a bright green.
- Continue to sauté for about 1 to 2 minutes and then remove the greens to a bowl. Serve hot.

Brazilian Rice *Chaval*

Rice is enjoyed every day in Brazil. It can be as simple or as elaborate as the cook makes it, but it is always a part of a Brazilian meal. This recipe involves a few more steps than ordinary boiled rice, but there is nothing every day about the results.

Serves 2 to 4

Ingredients

1 cup long-grain rice

1 garlic clove

1½ tablespoon vegetable oil

¾ teaspoon salt

1½ cups hot water

On your mark, get set . . .

- Place the rice in a fine mesh strainer and rinse with cold water. Skip the next three steps if you are using converted rice.
- Using your very clean hands or a spoon, swirl the rice as it rinses to remove any excess starch.
- Turn off the water and continue to stir the rice a bit more to help it drain. Give the strainer a few shakes to remove any additional water.
- Let the rice continue to drain while you prepare the rest of the recipe.
- Slightly crush the garlic by laying the flat side of a chef's knife on the clove and pressing evenly to break open the skin. Remove the skin, cut off the root end, and chop the garlic. Measure ½ tablespoon and set it aside.

Cook!

- In a 9- to 10-inch frying pan heat the oil over medium-heat high for 30 to 40 seconds.
- Once the oil is hot but not smoking, add the drained rice and garlic.
- Sauté for 4 to 5 minutes stirring the rice constantly to prevent it from sticking, or until all the rice has soaked up a bit of the oil and turned slightly darker.
- Add the hot water and salt.
- Return to a boil, lower the heat to simmer, cover the pan, and cook for about 18 minutes.
- Turn off the heat and let the pan rest, without raising the lid, for 5 to 10 minutes before serving. Fluff with a fork and serve.

Black Beans *Feijão Preto Simples*

Brazilians love beans. These tiny legumes show up in some form for almost every meal. Brazil grows red, brown, and white beans, but the black bean is by far the most popular. What is it about a perfectly prepared pot of beans with its enticing aroma and comforting flavor that makes them so popular? Why not try making some and find out for yourself?

Serves 4 to 6

Ingredients

1 pound black, kidney, or white dried beans
8 cups water
1 bay leaf
1 small red or yellow onion

1 garlic clove
1 tablespoon bacon fat or vegetable oil
1 teaspoon salt
1 to 2 sprigs cilantro, optional

On your mark, get set . . .

- Pour the beans, a few at a time, onto a clean baking tray or into a wide bowl. Carefully check for anything that is not a bean, such as pebbles, and discard.
- Pour the beans into a colander and rinse thoroughly with cold water. Using your very clean hands, swirl the beans around the colander to remove any dirt.
- Place the beans in a large pot, cover with the water, and let the beans soak for at least 6 hours or overnight.
- If you don't have enough time to soak the beans or you just want a quicker method, try this: Place the picked-over and washed beans in a large pot. Add the water and bring to a boil for 2 to 3 minutes. Turn the beans off, cover, and let stand for 1 to 1½ hours.

Cook!

- Rinse the soaked beans, add them to a large pot, and place them on the stove.
- Cover with enough cold water to come to 2 inches over the top of the beans. Add the bay leaf.
- Bring the beans to a boil over high heat, reduce the heat to low, and simmer for 1½ hours, or until the beans are tender.
- As the beans cook use a large spoon to remove any foam or impurities that rise to the surface.
- After 1 hour, remove and taste a few beans to determine their tenderness. They should be just soft without any trace of a hard center.

- Once the beans have cooked, peel and chop the onion into small pieces, measure 4 to 5 tablespoons, and set aside.
- Slightly crush the garlic by laying the flat side of a chef's knife on the clove and pressing evenly to break open the skin. Remove the skin, cut off the root end, and chop the garlic. Measure 1 tablespoon and set it aside.
- Place a 10-inch frying pan over medium heat and add the bacon fat or oil. Sauté the onion and garlic until soft. This will take 4 to 5 minutes. If they begin to brown, immediately lower the heat.
- Using a soup ladle or large spoon, transfer about 1 cup of the beans and a little of the liquid they were cooked in to the frying pan.
- Carefully mash the beans, using the back of the ladle or spoon to create a thick paste.

- Add the mashed bean paste to the large pot of simmering beans. Add the salt and the coriander leaves, and cook over medium-low for another 30 minutes.
- As the beans cook, mash them occasionally to help thicken the liquid. Serve hot.

Pepper and Lemon/Lime Sauce

Molho de Pimenta e Limão

This spicy sauce is the perfect accompaniment to many of the recipes in this book including Smoked Meat and Black Bean Stew (page 59), Roasted Pork Tenderloin (page 62), and Fish and Shrimp Stew (page 65). The sauce will keep for up to a week in the refrigerator.

Makes 1 cup

Ingredients

2 jalapeño or malagueta★ chile peppers or 1 tablespoon Tabasco sauce

1 small red or yellow onion

2 garlic cloves

1/2 teaspoon salt

1 lime or lemon

On your mark, get set . . .

- **Slip on a pair of kitchen gloves.**
- **Remove the stem from the chile and cut the chile in half. Rinse it under cold running water, scraping out and discarding the seeds. Cut the chiles into small pieces and place in a blender.**
- **Rinse, dry, and remove the gloves.**
- **Peel and finely chop the onion, measure 1/2 cup, and place in the blender.**
- **Slightly crush the garlic by laying the flat side of a chef's knife on the clove and pressing evenly to break open the skin. Remove the skin, cut off the root end, and chop the garlic. Measure 1 tablespoon and add to the blender.**
- **Add the salt to the blender as well.**
- **Squeeze the juice from the lime or lemon, measure 1/4 cup, and set aside for the moment.**

Blend!

- **Press the lid of the blender firmly into place.**
- **Turn the blender on and off a few times to break up the ingredients. Then, with the blender on high, gradually add the lime or lemon juice.**
- **Blend until the ingredients just come together into a thick sauce. Scrape the sauce into a bowl and let it stand at room temperature 30 minutes to 1 hour before serving.**

★*Malagueta peppers are available in South American specialty stores. Be careful! They are extremely hot.*

Brazilian Flavored Oil

Dendê palm oil is one of the main ingredients in many Brazilian dishes. It is available in specialty markets that sell South American ingredients. This recipe offers you a substitute for this oil, which might not be available in your area. It uses annatto seeds, popular in the cooking of Espírito Santo. The recipe also suggests alternate spices if annatto seeds are not available. The finished oil achieves not quite the same flavor as *dendê* oil, but it is delicious and will add a Brazilian flavor and color to the recipes in this book.

Makes 1 cup

Ingredients

1 cup extra-virgin olive oil
1 teaspoon ground annatto seeds or
 1/2 teaspoon each of paprika and
 ground turmeric

On your mark, get set . . .

- **Pour the oil into a medium-size pan.**
- **Add the spices and mix well with a small whisk.**
- **Fold the cheesecloth in thirds, place it in a fine mesh strainer, and put the strainer over a heat-proof bowl near the stove.**

Cook!

- **Place the pan over medium heat. Stir the oil occasionally to dissolve the spices.**
- **After about 3 to 4 minutes, small bubbles will begin to appear in the oil. As soon as that happens, turn the heat off and let the pan stand for 5 minutes.**
- **Strain the oil through the cheesecloth.**

- **Once the oil has cooled completely, pour into a clean glass jar with a tight-fitting lid, and store in the refrigerator until ready to use.**

Main Dishes

Smoked Meat and Black Bean Stew (page 59) with, upper left, Cheese Rolls (page 35) and, upper right, Sautéed Greens (page 45) and Brazilian Rice (page 47)

Colonial Chicken *Galinha Crioula*

The southernmost state of Rio Grande do Sul borders Argentina and Uruguay. Its cooking not only reflects these neighboring culinary influences but also those of the Italian and German immigrants, referred to by the Brazilians as "colonials." The Italians certainly left their mark on the cooking of the region, and this recipe with Parmesan cheese and plum tomatoes is a perfect example.

Serves 4

Ingredients

*1 3½ pound chicken, preferably organic
cut into 8 pieces
2 to 3 medium yellow onions
3 to 4 ripe plum tomatoes or 1 8-ounce can
chopped
2 garlic cloves
1 red bell pepper
1 cup long-grain rice*

*4 tablespoons vegetable oil or bacon fat
2 cups homemade Chicken Stock (page 22)
or canned low-sodium chicken broth
1½ teaspoons salt
½ teaspoon freshly ground black pepper
1 cup grated Parmesan cheese*

On your mark . . .

- **Wash then pat dry the chicken pieces.**
- **Lay the pieces on a cutting board and trim and discard any excess fat and skin.**
- **Put the chicken pieces in a bowl, cover with aluminum foil, and refrigerate while you prepare the rest of the ingredients.**
- **Wash the cutting board, knife, and your hands with lots of hot soapy water.**

Get set . . .

- **Peel the onions, cut them in half, and then chop each half into small chunks. Measure 2 cups and set aside.**
- **Wash the tomatoes. Cut out the stem circle at the top and discard. Cut the tomato in half then cut each half into small chunks. Measure 2 cups and set aside.**
- **Slightly crush the garlic by laying the flat side of a chef's knife on the clove and pressing evenly to break open the skin. Remove the skin, cut off the root end, and chop the garlic. Measure 1 tablespoon and set it aside.**
- **Wash the bell pepper and cut out the stem at the top.**
- **Cut the pepper in half and remove the seeds and white membrane.**

- Cut each half into long strips and then roughly chop the strips into chunks. Measure 1 cup and set it aside.

- Pour the rice into a fine mesh strainer or colander and rinse thoroughly with cold water. Swirl the rice around as it rinses to help remove any starch, then let it drain.

Cook!

- Heat 2 tablespoon of the oil in a 10- to 12-inch heavy-bottomed or cast-iron frying pan over medium heat for 30 to 40 seconds.
- When the oil is hot but not smoking, add the chicken and brown on both sides. This will take about 15 minutes. Don't overcrowd the pan. If necessary, do this step in two batches, adding more oil as needed.

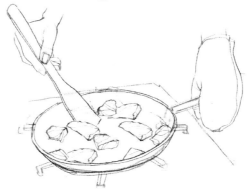

- Once the chicken is browned, remove the pieces to a clean platter and ask your adult to drain off all but about 1 tablespoon of the oil.
- Add the garlic and sauté for 30 seconds. Add the onions and bell pepper, and sauté for 2 minutes. Return the chicken pieces to the pan.
- Turn the heat to medium-high, and add the tomatoes and the 2 cups of broth. Season with the salt and pepper.
- Once the pan comes to a boil, cover it leaving the lid slightly ajar, and reduce the heat to low. Cook for 20 minutes.

- After 20 minutes, add the rice, gently stirring it into the liquid.
- Turn the heat to medium-high and bring the liquid to a boil.
- Once it boils, cover the pan, reduce the heat to low, and cook for an additional 20 to 25 minutes or until all the liquid is absorbed.
- Ask your adult assistant to turn on the oven broiler.
- Remove the lid from the chicken and evenly sprinkle the grated cheese over the top.
- Ask your adult assistant to place the chicken under the broiler for 1 to 2 minutes, or until the cheese melts and turns golden brown. Watch the chicken closely so that it does not burn.
- Bring the chicken to the table in the frying pan and serve piping hot with Sautéed Greens (page 45).

Smoked Meat and Black Bean Stew

Feijoada Completa

If there is any recipe in Brazilian cooking designed to bring people together it is *feijoada*, the national dish of Brazil. This version comes from the city of Rio de Janeiro. Traditionally served on Saturday afternoon, this rich, dark, smoky-flavored stew is essential for creating a Brazilian feast! It is traditionally served with Sautéed Greens (page 45), Brazilian Rice (page 47), and plenty of sliced oranges. *Feijoada* takes time to make, so plan ahead. Read the recipe carefully first to understand all the steps involved. Then you'll find it easy to prepare.

Serves 10 to 12

Ingredients

2 pounds black beans

Smoked Meats:
Select 1 pound each of 3 smoked meats:
chorizo, linguica, smoked kielbasa or other
smoked sausage, pepperoni, smoked pork (ribs,
loin, or chops), smoked pork hocks, smoked
beef tongue, lean slab bacon, Canadian bacon,
or smoked ham (all preferably in one piece)

3 cloves garlic
2 medium yellow onions
½ bunch flat-leaf parsley
5 to 6 sprigs cilantro
2 tablespoons extra-virgin olive oil

Fresh Meats:
Select 1 pound each of 2 fresh meats:
beef sirloin or chuck (cut into 2 pieces),
Italian sausage, or country-style pork ribs

3 tablespoons olive oil
1 bay leaf
1 teaspoon ground cumin
5 oranges, preferably organic

On your mark, get set . . .

- **Pour the beans on a clean baking tray or into a wide bowl. Carefully check for anything that is not a bean, such as pebbles, and discard.**
- **Place the beans in a colander and wash thoroughly with cold water. Using your very clean hands, swirl the beans around the colander to remove any dirt. Place the beans in a large bowl and cover with the water.**
- **Let the beans soak for at least 6 hours or overnight.**
- **If you want a quicker method, place the picked-over and washed beans in a large pot. Add the water and bring to a boil. Boil for 2 to 3 minutes. Turn the beans off, cover, and let stand for 1 to 1 ½ hours.**

- Wash all of the smoked meats, except the sausages and/or pepperoni, in plenty of cold water, and then place them in a large bowl.
- Pour in enough cold water to cover the meats by 2 inches, cover with plastic wrap or aluminum foil, and refrigerate for 4 hours or overnight.
- Change the water once or twice during the soaking to help remove the extra salt from the meats.

Cook!

- Drain the soaked beans in a colander.

- Place them in a pot large enough to hold the beans and all the meat.
- Add the smoked meats, except the sausages and/or pepperoni, which will go in later, and add the fresh meats to the pot along with the beans.
- Cover with enough cold water to measure 3 inches above the meat and bring it to a boil over high heat. Skim any foam or impurities that rise to the surface. You will need to do this several times during cooking.

- Once the beans boil, reduce the heat to low and simmer for 1 1/2 hours, or until the beans and meat are tender. Continue to skim the pot as needed, and stir the pot occasionally to keep it from sticking.
- About 15 minutes before the beans have finished cooking, slightly crush the garlic by laying the flat side of a chef's knife on the clove and pressing evenly to break open the skin. Remove the skin, cut off the root end, and chop the garlic. Measure 1 tablespoon and set it aside.

- Peel the onions and cut them in half. Cut each half into 1/4-inch-thick slices, roughly chop the slices, measure 1 1/2 cups, and set aside.
- Wash the parsley and cilantro thoroughly in cold water to remove any sand, shake off the excess moisture, and wrap in paper towels to absorb any remaining moisture.
- Roughly chop the cilantro and parsley together, measure 1/2 to 3/4 cup and set aside.
- Heat the oil in a large skillet over medium for 30 to 40 seconds, and add the garlic, onions, parsley, and cilantro and sauté for 5 minutes. If the mixture begins to brown, lower the heat.
- Scoop up about two ladles of hot beans, along with a little of the cooking liquid, and add it to the vegetables. Using the back of the ladle, mash the beans to help thicken the liquid. Cook for 5 to 7 minutes.

- Return the beans to the pot. Wash one of the oranges thoroughly under cold water. Add it whole to the pot along with any sausage and/or pepperoni you are using. Stir well to combine and cook for another 40 minutes.
- When you are ready to serve, remove and discard the whole orange.
- Separate the meats from the beans using a slotted spoon. Cut the meats into serving sizes and arrange them on a large platter. Spoon a little of the bean liquid over the meats to keep them moist.
- Serve the beans in a covered dish, along with Sautéed Greens (page 45), Brazilian Rice (page 47), Cheese Rolls (page 35), and Pepper and Lemon/Lime Sauce (page 50).
- Slice the remaining oranges into 1/4-inch-thick slices and arrange on a serving dish.
- Serve hot.

Roasted Pork Tenderloin

Lombo de Porco Assado

When Brazilians think of their favorite way to prepare pork, this recipe might be the first to spring to mind. Originally from the state of Minas Gerais, this dish is a Brazilian classic. Plan ahead when you decide to cook this recipe. The pork needs to marinate for several hours or overnight. But after the initial step of marinating, the recipe is easy to prepare.

Serves 4 to 6

Ingredients

1 3-pound boneless center-cut pork loin
2 to 3 oranges
1 lime
1 medium yellow onion
2 garlic cloves

1 bay leaf
1 small bunch flat-leaf parsley
8 black peppercorns
1 teaspoon salt
4 to 5 green onions

On your mark, get set . . .

- Rinse the pork under cold running water and pat dry with paper towels.
- Place it in a bowl or pan just large enough to accommodate it and set it aside.
- Cut the oranges in half, squeeze the juice, and remove any seeds. Measure 1 cup of juice and pour it into a blender.
- Cut the lime in half, squeeze the juice, and add it to the blender.
- Peel and roughly chop the onion and add it to the blender as well.
- Peel and chop the garlic and add it to the blender.
- Crush the bay leaf and add it to the blender.
- Wash the parsley and shake off any excess water. Set aside 8 to 10 sprigs, wrap the remainder in paper towels, and set it aside for later use.
- Remove the stems from the parsley sprigs and roughly chop the leaves, measure 1/4 cup, and add to the blender along with the salt and pepper. Blend at high speed for 30 seconds. This is the marinade.
- Pour the marinade over the pork and, using a spoon, baste the entire roast with it.
- Cover the bowl with aluminum foil and refrigerate the pork for at least 6 hours or overnight.

Cook!

- Preheat the oven to 375°F.
- Remove the marinated meat from the refrigerator.

- Lightly oil a roasting pan just large enough to hold the roast.
- Lift the meat out of the marinade, lay it in the roasting pan, and reserve the marinade. You should have a total of about 1⅓ cups.
- Place the meat in the pan and roast on the middle rack of the oven for 25 minutes.
- After 25 minutes, pour about ⅓ of the reserved marinade over the roasting meat and continue to cook for another 1½ hours, basting the meat every 30 minutes or so, with the pan drippings and the reserved marinade, until all the marinade has been used.
- Use a meat thermometer to be sure the meat has reached an internal temperature of 160 to 165°F and is done. Remove it from the oven and let it rest for 10 minutes. In the meantime, skim and discard any fat from the surface of the pan drippings.
- Wash the green onion, remove any dark or discolored leaves, chop into thin slices, measure ½ cup, and set aside.
- Remove the reserved parsley from the refrigerator, wash, drain, chop, and measure 3 tablespoons.
- Heat the skimmed pan drippings over medium heat, add the chopped green onion and parsley, and sauté for 1 to 2 minutes. This is the sauce. If needed, you can add a little hot water, orange or lime juice if the sauce is too thick.
- Cut the pork into slices and arrange them on a platter. Spoon some of the sauce over the slices and serve along with Black Beans (page 48), Sautéed Greens (page 45), and Brazilian Rice (page 47).

Fish and Shrimp Stew *Moqueca Capixaba*

This fish and shrimp stew comes from Espírito Santo where *moqueca capixaba* is a legendary dish. It is traditionally cooked in a covered earthenware pot. A heavy-bottomed frying pan with a lid makes an excellent substitute. When shopping for this recipe, look for the freshest fish available. The freshness of the fish will make a big difference in the flavor of the dish. You may use frozen shrimp but make sure they are completely thawed before starting to cook.

Serves 4

Ingredients

2 pounds boneless fresh cod or turbot fillets or
  combination of both★
1½ teaspoons salt
½ pound large fresh or fully thawed frozen
  shrimp
2 garlic cloves
3 ripe plum tomatoes

1 medium onion
2 limes
8 to 10 sprigs cilantro
3 to 4 green onions
2½ tablespooons Brazilian Flavored Oil
  (page 51) or extra-virgin olive oil
¼ cup clam juice

On your mark . . .

- **Rinse the fish fillets then pat dry.**
- **Check for bones by laying the fillets over an inverted bowl. Slowly run your very clean hands over the surface of the fillet to feel for any bones and removing any you find. A clean pair of needle-nose pliers is a good tool for pulling them out, or you can use a clean piece of paper towel to grip the tip of the bone and pull it free.**

- Once you have removed any bones, cut each fillet into 3 equal portions. You will have a total of 6 pieces.

- Lay the fish pieces in a bowl, sprinkle with 1 teaspoon of salt, and refrigerate them while you prepare the rest of the ingredients.
- Wash and dry the cutting board, knife, and your hands.
- Carefully peel off the shells and the tails of the shrimp.
- Remove the vein from the shrimp. To do this, lay the shrimp on a cutting board. Using a paring knife, make a slight cut down the back about 1/4 inch deep, starting at the widest end or the top the shrimp.
- As you cut, you will see a black vein. Rinse the shrimp under cold running water, and pull out and discard the vein. Repeat with the rest of the shrimp. Place the shrimp in a bowl and refrigerate.

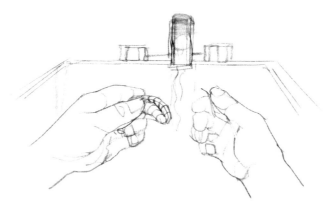

Get set . . .

- Slightly crush the garlic by laying the flat side of a chef's knife on the clove and pressing evenly to break open the skin. Remove the skin, cut off the root end, and chop the garlic. Measure 1 tablespoon and set it aside.
- Wash the tomatoes. Cut out the stem circle at the top and discard.
- Cut the tomato in half then cut each half into small chunks. Measure 2 cups, and set aside.

- Peel and chop the onion into small chunks, measure 2 cups, and set aside.
- Cut the lime in half, squeeze the juice, measure 1/3 cup, and set aside.
- Wash the cilantro to remove any dirt or sand. Shake off the excess water, roughly chop, measure 1/3 cup, and set aside.
- Wash the green onions, cut off the stem end, remove any dark or discolored leaves, then chop the white tips and about 2 inches of the green stems into 1/4-inch pieces.
- Measure 1/4 cup green onions and set aside.

Cook!

- Remove the fish and shrimp from the refrigerator.
- Have the rest of the ingredients close to the stove.
- Heat 2 tablespoons of the oil in a 10- to 12-inch frying pan for 30 to 40 seconds over medium heat.
- When the oil is hot but not smoking, add the garlic and sauté for 1 minute.
- Add 1 cup each of the chopped tomatoes and chopped onions. Sauté for 2 to 3 minutes.
- Lay the pieces of fish and shrimp on top of the onions and tomatoes in a single layer.

- Sprinkle 1 teaspoon of salt over the fish. Pour the lime juice over the seafood combination, then spoon on the remaining tomatoes and onions to form an even layer over the top.
- Sprinkle the cilantro over the tomatoes, add the green onions, and then pour the remaining 1 1/2 tablespoons of oil evenly over the fish and shrimp.
- Add the clam juice. Don't stir the ingredients.
- Cover the pan, reduce the heat to low, and cook for 10 to 15 minutes or until the shrimp are bright pink and the fish is cooked through and tender.
- Serve the stew hot with rice.

★ *You may also use any other firm-fleshed fish such as mahi mahi, grouper, red snapper, or wild salmon.*

Desserts

From left: Brazilian Birthday Candies (page 72) and Brazil Nut Cookies (page 70)

Brazil Nut Cookies
Biscoitinho de Castanha do Pará

What is more Brazilian than cookies made from Amazonian Brazil nuts? This recipe uses a food processor so ask your adult assistant to help with those steps. These cookies will have your guests begging for more, so luckily for you this recipe can be doubled.

Makes 24 cookies

Ingredients

1½ cups granulated sugar
1 cup white cornmeal
*1 cup all-purpose flour plus 2 teaspoons
  for dusting cookie sheet*

*2 sticks unsalted butter at room temperature,
  plus 1 teaspoon for cookie sheet*
1 cup Brazil nuts

On your mark, get set . . .

- Measure 1 cup of the sugar and place it in a large bowl.
- Place the other 1/2 cup of sugar in a small bowl and set aside.
- Add the white cornmeal and flour to the 1 cup of sugar, blend well, and set aside.
- Lightly spread the teaspoon of butter over the surface of a cookie sheet. Your very clean fingertips work best.
- Sprinkle the 2 teaspoons of flour over the surface of the cookie sheet.
- Lift the cookie sheet up from one end and tip it back and forth tapping it on the countertop to help the flour evenly coat the entire surface.
- Turn the tray upside down over the sink and give it a gentle whack to remove any excess flour, then set the cookie sheet aside. Be careful not to touch the surface once you have buttered and floured it.
- Ask your adult assistant to help with the next few steps that use a food processor.
- Put the Brazil nuts in a food processor.
- Cut 1 stick of the butter into 1/4-inch slices and add to the nuts. Add about *1/2* of the flour-and-sugar combination on top of the nuts and butter.
- Cut the second stick of butter into 1/4-inch slices and add them to the processor.
- Now add the remainder of the flour combination on top as a final layer.
- Put the lid on and pulse on and off 20 times, and then let the processor run for 20 seconds. This will bring all the ingredients together into a soft dough.
- Empty the dough into a large bowl. Carefully lift out the blade and scrape out any dough that may be stuck to bottom of the processor. Add it to the rest of the dough.

- Using a rubber spatula, give the dough a few stirs.
- Refrigerate the dough for 20 to 30 minutes.

Cook!

- **Preheat the oven to 350° F.**
- Wash and dry your hands.
- Using a teaspoon, scoop up a generous teaspoonful of the dough and place it in the palm of your hand.
- Gently form the dough into the size of 1-inch ball. Don't worry if the dough balls are not round, as they will shape themselves as they bake.
- Roll the ball of dough in the 1/2 cup of reserved sugar evenly coating it, and then place it on the baking sheet. Leave about 1/2 inch of space between each cookie.
- Bake the cookies for 30 minutes or until lightly browned.
- Remove the cookie sheet from the oven and let the cookies cool undisturbed on the baking sheet for 5 minutes.
- Using a spatula, carefully lift the cookies off the sheet onto a cooling rack and let them cool completely.
- Store in an airtight container.

Brazilian Birthday Candies

Brigadeiro

Is someone's birthday coming up? Well if you live in Brazil and it's your special day, chances are you would find these colorful treats in abundant supply at the birthday celebration. Even if it's not your birthday, try this recipe anyway. These candies have such a reputation among Brazilians that they say if you make *brigadeiro* for someone who is feeling bad, chances are you can make them smile. Just make sure you get these bright delights to the party before you sample too many, so your guests get to enjoy them, too.

Makes about 20

Ingredients

1 can sweetened condensed milk
2 tablespoons unsweetened cocoa powder
1 teaspoon corn syrup
2 teaspoons salted butter
1/2 cup multicolored candy sprinkles for cake decorating

On your mark, get set . . .

- Combine the condensed milk, unsweetened cocoa powder, and corn syrup in a 2-quart heavy-bottomed saucepan.
- Stir until well combined and then place on the stove.
- Lightly butter a 10- to 12-inch oval platter or large dish with 1/4 teaspoon of the butter and set it aside.

Cook!

- Heat the milk, cocoa, and corn syrup over medium heat, stirring constantly with a wooden spoon until the mixture starts to form small bubbles around the outside. This will take about 4 minutes.
- Once it starts to boil, reduce the heat to low, and add 1 teaspoon of the butter.
- Continue stirring until the mixture thickens and begins to pull away from the sides and bottom of the pan. The mixture will thicken quickly, and if you don't keep stirring, it will stick to the bottom of the pan.
- Cook for 3 to 4 minutes, stirring frequently.
- Pour the contents of the pan onto the platter and spread it evenly across the surface until it is about 1/3 inch thick.
- Refrigerate for 15 minutes. Set a timer so you don't forget.

- In the meantime pour the sprinkles into a medium-size bowl or 8 1/2-inch bread pan. Be prepared. Forming the candies is a messy operation, so take your time and wear an apron.
- After 15 minutes, remove the platter from the refrigerator. Take some of the remaining butter and lightly spread a bit of it into the palms of your hands.
- Scoop up about 1 teaspoon of the candy, and roll it into a ball in the palms of your hands, then drop the candy into the colored sprinkles. Now, shake the pan back and forth until the entire surface of the ball is completely covered with sprinkles.
- Place the completed candy on a serving dish and continue until all the candies are rolled and coated.
- Cover the *brigadeiro* with aluminum foil, being careful that the foil does not touch the candy and stick to it.
- Refrigerate until ready to serve. These candies can be frozen and served ice cold as well.

Helpful Kitchen Equipment and Utensils

CUTTING BOARD

ASSORTED KNIVES

VEGETABLE PEELER

SAUCEPANS WITH LIDS

STOCKPOT WITH LID

SPATULA

WHISK

BAKING PAN

ELECTRIC MIXER

MIXING BOWL

LADLE

LARGE METAL SPOON

COOKIE SHEET

SMALL HAND STRAINER

FOUR-SIDED GRATER

COLANDER

JUICER

CHEESECLOTH

MORTAR AND PESTLE

FRYING PAN

FOOD PROCESSOR

CAKE PAN

COFFEE/SPICE GRINDER

ESSENTIAL INGREDIENTS IN THE BRAZILIAN KITCHEN

BREAD CRUMBS

The best bread crumbs are the ones you make yourself. Old bread that has dried out is ideal for making really good crumbs. Grate it with a hand grater, using the tiniest holes. Be careful not to grate your knuckles along with the bread. You can also buy bread crumbs. Look for the ones marked "plain." They will have no salt or extra seasoning. That way you can season them yourself.

CHILE PEPPERS, FRESH

Jalapeño peppers are an excellent substitute for Brazilian peppers. Jalapeños are green or red in color, with the red being generally milder. It is important when handling chiles, dried or fresh, to wear latex kitchen gloves and to wash and dry the gloves after you are done handling the chiles. Never touch your eyes, nose, or any other part of your face to prevent contact with the hot oils that are found naturally in chiles.

CILANTRO

Cilantro is an herb also known as fresh coriander or Chinese parsley. It adds great flavor to Brazilian dishes. Cilantro looks almost identical to parsley and is easily confused with it, but it has a bolder flavor and a stronger aroma. Cilantro should be washed to remove any dirt still clinging to the stems or leaves. Wrapped in paper towels and then in a plastic bag, it will keep for about a week in the refrigerator.

COCONUT MILK

Coconut milk is a common ingredient in the dishes that come from the state of Bahia. Many people are concerned about the fat content of coconut milk and select a "lite" or "ultra-lite" version. The choice is yours as any of the unsweetened varieties will work. Canned coconut cream is also available, and its fat content, like real cream, is higher than that of milk.

CLOVES

A clove is the tiny dried flower bud from an evergreen tree. It comes whole or ground. If you buy it whole and grind it yourself, you're assured of the best flavor. It should be used carefully because the flavor of cloves can overpower the other elements in your recipe.

CUMIN

The cumin seed, a member of the parsley family, is a familiar spice in Brazilian cooking and is used either whole or ground.

DENDÊ PALM OIL

Thick, dense, and orange, *dendê* palm oil is extracted from the nuts of an African palm tree. It is high is vitamin A and has a delectable flavor and aroma. It is very high in saturated fat, so you should carefully consider that before using it. It is an essential ingredient in the cooking of the state of Bahia and is used throughout Brazil as well. It can only be found in stores that specialize in South American or African ingredients or through the Internet. Use the recipe for Brazilian Flavored Oil (page 51) as a substitute.

GARLIC

Garlic is a member of the onion family and a valuable flavor maker in Brazilian cooking. When you purchase garlic, look for large bulbs that are hard and solid. The bulb is composed of cloves. To use the cloves, first separate them from the bulb. With the flat side of a knife, give them a good whack, then remove the white paperlike skin and cut off the dark tip. The cloves can then be chopped into small pieces, mashed, or cut into thin slices. Many nutritionists believe that garlic has great health benefits because it is rich in minerals.

MANIOC FLOUR OR MEAL

Manioc is also known as cassava. It is a root vegetable native to Central and South America. Manioc meal or flour is made after the tuber has been washed and processed and the juice has been extracted. The ground root is more commonly known in North America as tapioca starch or tapioca flour. You will probably find it in health-food stores or markets that specialize in South American products.

PARSLEY, FRESH FLAT-LEAF

This variety of parsley is full of flavor. Look for bright green leaves and stems that are not wilted or shriveled. Be sure you don't make a common mistake and buy coriander, a similar-looking herb, by mistake. Wash the parsley before you use it, wrap it in paper towels to absorb excess moisture, and then chop it.

TOMATOES

Tomatoes are a key ingredient in many Brazilian dishes. When shopping for fresh tomatoes, look for a nice rich, red color and avoid the fruits with spots or bruises. If you are unable to find good fresh tomatoes, don't hesitate to buy canned. To store fresh tomatoes, keep them away from heat, but never put them in the refrigerator. The cold will destroy their flavor and texture.

TURMERIC

Dried turmeric root is ground into a golden powder. Be careful when using turmeric because it will stain and the stains are not easy to remove. That is probably why it is used as a fabric dye as well as a spice. It is a good idea to use a spoon to mix or coat other ingredients with turmeric so you keep it on the food and not you.

INDEX

Map, 11

African influence, 12, 15
Amazon River, 14
Amerindians, 10, 15
Appetizers
    miniature meat pies, 39–41

Bahia, 15. *See also* Hearts of palm
    salad; Miniature meat pies
Beaches, 13
Belém, 15
Black beans *(Feijão preto simples)*,
    48–49
Brazilian birthday candies *(Brigadeiro)*,
    72–73
Brazilian rice *(Chaval)*, 47
Brazil nut cookies *(Biscoitinho de cas-*
    tanha do Pará), 70–71
Breads and rolls
    cheese rolls, 35–37

Candy, 72–73
Cheese rolls *(Pão de queijo)*, 35–37
Chicken soup *(Canja de galinha)*,
    19–21
Chicken stock *(Caldo de galinha)*,
    22–23
Churrasc, 14
Cleaning, 6–7
Coconut milk, 76
Colonial chicken *(Galinha crioula)*,
    55–57
Condiments and flavorings, 15, 50, 51,
    76–77
Cutting, 7

Dairy and cheese, 13
    in Brazilian birthday can-
        dies, 72–73
    in cheese rolls, 35–37
    in colonial chicken,
        55–57
    in miniature meat pies,
        39–41
Desserts

birthday candies, 72–73
Brazil nut cookies, 70–71
Espíritu Santo, 13. *See also* Fish and
    shrimp stew
Etiquette, 15
European influence, 10, 13, 55

Fish and seafood, 13, 15
    fish and shrimp stew, 65–67
    shrimp and black-eyed pea salad,
        29–31
    substitutions, 29, 67
Fish and shrimp stew *(Moqueca capixaba)*,
    65–67
Fruits, 13, 15. *See also* Tomatoes
    oranges, 59, 62
    pepper and lemon/lime sauce, 50

Garlic, 77
Gauchos, 13–14
Grains and rice
    Brazilian rice, 47
    in colonial chicken, 55–57
    corn meal
        in Brazil nut cookies, 70–71
    manioc (cassava), 15, 77
        in cheese rolls, 35–37
        in smoked meat and black
            bean stew, 59–61
    wagoner's rice, 13
Grating, 8

Hearts of palm salad *(Salada de
    palmito)*, 32–33
Holidays, 10. *See also* Brazilian birthday
    candies

Ingredients, 15, 47, 48, 76–77

Local products, 13, 15

Main courses
    roasted pork tenderloin, 62–63
    smoked meat and black bean stew,
        59–61
Main dishes
    colonial chicken, 55–57
    fish and shrimp stew, 65–67
    roasted pork tenderloin, 62–63

smoked meat and black bean
    stew, 59–61
Manioc (cassava), 15, 77. *See also*
    Cheese rolls
Meat
    miniature meat pies, 39–41
    preserved, 13–14
    roasted pork tenderloin, 62–63
    salted and sun-dried, 13
    sausage, 14, 59–61
    smoked meat and black bean
        stew, 59–61
    Minas Gerais, 13. *See also*
        Cheese rolls; Chicken
        soup; Roasted pork tender
        loin; Sautéed greens
    Miniature meat pies *(Pastel de
        carne)*, 39–41

Northern regions, 14–15. *See also*
    Brazil nut cookies; Chicken
    soup; Hearts of palm salad;
    Miniature meat pies
Nuts, 15
    Brazil nut cookies, 70–71
    in hearts of palm
        salad, 32–33

Oils *(dendê)*, 15, 51, 77

Pará, 15. *See also* Brazil nut cookies
Paraná, 13
Poultry
    chicken soup, 19–21
    chicken stock, 22–23
    colonial chicken, 55–57

Restaurants, 14
    Rio de Janeiro, 10–12. See also
        Smoked meat and
        black bean stew
Rio Grande do Sul, 14. *See also*
    Colonial Chicken
Roasted pork tenderloin *(Lombo de
    porco assado)*, 62–63
Safety, 6–7, 77
Salads
    hearts of palm, 32–33

shrimp and black-eyed pea
    salad, 29–31
São Paulo, 12–13. *See also* Shrimp
    and black-eyed pea salad
Saturdays, 10–12
Sauces
    pepper and lemon/lime, 50
Sautéed greens (*Couve à mineira*), 45
Sautéing, 8
Shopping, 76, 77
Shrimp and black-eyed pea salad
(*Salada de feijão fradinho com camarão*),
    29–31
Simmering, 9
Skewers, 14
Skimming, 9
Smoked meat and black bean stew
    (*Feijoada completa*), 10–12,
    59–61

Soups and stocks
    black bean soup, 25
    chicken soup, 19–21
    chicken stock, 22–23
Southern regions, 10–14. *See also*
    Brazilian rice; Cheese rolls;
        Colonial chicken;
        Fish and shrimp stew;
        Roasted pork ten
        derloin; Sautéed greens;
        Shrimp and black-eyed
        pea salad; Smoked meat
        and black bean stew
Stains, 77
Substitutions
    annato seeds, 51
    oil, 51
    peppers, 76
    salt cod, 29, 67

Techniques, 8, 9, 14
Tomatoes
    buying and storing, 77
    in colonial chicken,
        55–57
    in fish and shrimp stew,
        65–67
    in hearts of palm salad,
        32–33
    in miniature meat pies, 39–41

Utensils, 7, 74–75

Vegetables. See also Tomatoes
    black beans, 25, 48–49, 59–61
    black-eyes peas, 29–31
    hearts of palm, 32–33
    sautéed greens, 45

METRIC CONVERSION CHART

You can use the chart below to convert from U.S. measurements to the metric system.

Weight
1 ounce = 28 grams
1/2 pound (8 ounces) = 227 grams
1 pound = .45 kilograms
2.2 pounds = 1 kilogram

Liquid volume
1 teaspoon = 5 milliliters
1 tablespoon = 15 milliliters
1 fluid ounce = 30 milliliters
1 cup = 240 milliliters (.24 liters)
1 pint = 480 milliliters (.48 liters)
1 quart = .95 liter

Length
1/4 inch = .6 centimeter
1/2 inch = 1.25 centimeters
1 inch = 2.5 centimeters

Temperature
100°F = 40°C
110°F = 45°C
212°F = 100°C (boiling point of water)
350°F = 180°C
375°F = 190°C
400°F = 200°C
425°F = 220°C
450°F = 235°C

(To convert temperatures in Fahrenheit to Celsius, subtract 32 and multiply by .56)